Purposeful (Not Random) Acts of Kindness

(AKA Beginning Steps for Overcoming Spoiled Brat-aholism)

Garie Thomas-Bass, BA, EX, CX
Dr. Kertia Thomas-Black, MD
Kirtis Thomas III, LLP LPC

PublishAmerica
Baltimore

© 2007 by Garie Thomas-Bass, BA, EX, CX, Dr. Kertia Thomas-Black, MD, and Kirtis Thomas III, LLP LPC.
All rights reserved. No part of this book may be reproduced, stored in a retrieval system, or transmitted in any form or by any means without the prior written permission of the publishers, except by a reviewer who may quote brief passages in a review to be printed in a newspaper, magazine, or journal.

First printing

ISBN: 1-4241-7958-0
PUBLISHED BY PUBLISHAMERICA, LLLP
www.publishamerica.com
Baltimore

Printed in the United States of America

Dear reader,

Warning!!!
We are going to be using some VERY strong, and to some sensibilities, harsh words throughout this book, especially at the section of the book we honestly called "SKULL" (standing for skull and cross bones). Therefore, if you are easily offended or if your feelings are hurt readily, may we kindly suggest that you:

PUT THIS BOOK DOWN NOW!!! (or at least avoid reading the SKULL section on each of the pages)

These first few pages will be the ONLY "politically correct" warning that you will receive. This book is NOT for the pseudo (or real, for that matter) Dr. Spock advocates.

NOTE: Since this disclaimer is being rendered, if you continue to read this book, the consequences are YOUR responsibility! PLEASE do not write, call, nor e-mail us to complain. As stated above, you should NOT read this book in the first place if you are easily upset.

In addition, if you hate reading or hearing words or phrases that deal with things like rules, discipline, responsibility, changing behavior, conserving, sharing, or cooperating, to name a few, then I strongly suggest that you stop and run away from this book immediately.

On the other hand, if you are one of the folk who is sick and tired of all of the chaos, meanness, and selfish/self-indulgent behavior that we, in this book will refer to as "brat-aholism," you have come to the correct place. READ ON!

This book is dedicated to our mom, Mrs. Rose Mae Thomas. She was the inspiration, teacher, and wonderful example of a fantastic, giving, loving, strong, and co-operative life. Throughout her lifetime, she actually modeled and spoke to us about some of the concrete concepts that are used in this book.

Sadly, she passed away on July 13, 2003. She would have been very proud to see this book. We know she would have gotten several laughs from it, too.

God bless your soul, Mom.

Acknowledgements

Thank you words for family:
Garie would like to thank her husband, Paul Bass, for his consistent faith, love and encouragement.
Kertia would like to especially thank her husband, Sidney, and her children, Kareem and Christine, for their love and support.
Kirtis would like to thank his wife, Jeanne Thomas, for her continuous love, encouragement, and care.
Thank you to our sister, Bertha Thomas, and brother, Kabin Thomas and their family members (Patrick, Joshua, Alexander, Olivia, and Kabin Andrew) for their positive energy, loyalty and patience.
We would also like to say thank you to our Aunt Margueritte Russell (our mom's sister) for her strength, gentle nature and courage.

Many thank you words to other authors:
Gail Hershenzon (good friend, author, wonderful teacher, and fellow recycler) for all of her encouragement, hard work and enthusiasm; Antonio Cassone (friend and creative author and entertainer) for the help and direction with the steps for the publishing of our book; Paul Kavieff (well-known author and engineer) for his wisdom and generosity in helping us with publishing and book proposal information.

A BIG thank you for the spiritual influences of:
Bishop Thomas Gumbleton (pastor of St. Leo Catholic Church in Detroit, Michigan) for his dedication to walking in the real light of truth despite the cost; Reverend Greg Barrette (senior minister of Renaissance Unity Church in Warren, Michigan) for his (and the church's entire ministerial team's) motivational messages; Reverend Richard Beattie (Renaissance Unity) for his many prayers and words of support after our mom made her transition; Reverend Linda McCall (Unity minister, teacher, and friend) for her support and for her example of determination and goal achieving; Father Jerome Singer and Sr. Jolene Van Handel (both of Nativity Catholic Church, also in Detroit, which was our mom's former church—she loved attending Nativity!) for their warmth, care, and respect-filled welcome of our mom for so many years.

Acknowledgements

Thank you very much to all of our friends and role models (some we have known since elementary school). We wish we had the space to name ALL of you. If we miss you in this book, we will put more names in our next book (Honest!).

Douglas Fogelman, thank you for being such an intelligent and dedicated person in the struggle and you are a very patient listener too; Phil Schloop, thank you for all your hard work and encouragement; Judy Dlugosielski and Teddi Barnes, thank you for your compassion and loyalty; Sr. Jonathon (Sandy) Shipp, thank you for being a wonderful example of the philosophy of St. Francis of Assisi. Thank you for sharing your wonderful voice in music and for being an excellent educator.

Ruby Windhom, thank you for your energy and inspiration; Connice (Wilcox) Ross, thank you for your calm grace, wonderful sense of humor, and consistent faith; Margie Tate, thank you for your understanding and especially thank you for reminding us that Faith, Family, and Friends are the most important foundations of a good life.

The pages of this book are made of 50% recycled paper content.

The authors have made a pledge to personally donate 10% of the profits from the sale of this book to The American Society for the Preventions of Cruelty to Animals (ASPCA). Please note that PublishAmerica.com does not handle this type of transaction. If you have questions or suggestions on this issue please feel free to contact the authors at purposefulnotrandom.com.

TABLE OF CONTENTS   RULE #

AGE
   -Asking (Don't)   1

ANIMALS/PET
   -Barking (Stop)   2
   -Curbing (Do—and every time)   3
   -Spay/Neuter (Just do it!)   4

ARGUING
   -In public (Ignorant behavior)   5

ATM/TELLER MACHINES
   -Cleaning up (Do)   6
   -Distance (Back up)   7
   -Preparation (Always)   8

BABIES/CHILDREN
   -Accompanying (Always)   9
   -Compliments (Careful)   10
   -Crawling (Where)   11
   -Cursing (Never)   12
   -ID (Claim them)   13
   -Religious services (No)   14
   -Theatres (Not)   15

CHURCH
   -Talking (No! No!)   16

CLOTHING
   -Slippers (Never outside)   17

COURTESY
   -Compliments (Don't beg)   18
   -Visitors (Keep them safe)   19

TABLE OF CONTENTS   RULE #

DOORS
  -Opening (Don't let them slam)   20
  -Thank you (Always)   21

DRIVEE
  -Promptness (Always)   22

DRIVING
  -Conversation (Eyes forward)   23
  -Distance (Not so close, buddy)   24
  -Gratitude (Ungrateful)   25
  -Merging (Take your turn)   26
  -Pulling over to the side (Move out of the way!)   27

EARS
  -Public cleaning (YUCKY)   28

EATING
  -Food in mouth (Keep it to yourself)   29

ELEVATORS
  -Speaking when you step in (Are we invisible?)   30

EMBARRASSING MOMENTS
  -Inform people (Have some guts)   31

GUM
  -Disposal (Use your brain)   32

LINES
  -Completing transactions (Move!)   33

LIPS
  -Closed (Close them!)   34

TABLE OF CONTENTS   RULE

MUSIC
 -Volume (Turn it down!)   35

NAILS
 -Public clipping (Raised in a barn)   36

PAGE TURNING
 -Finger licking (Burn the book)   37

PHONE
 -Answering (People matter)   38
 -Cell phone (You're not special)   39
 -Messages (Keep it simple, stupid)   40
 -Wrong number (Let them know)   41

SHOPPING CARTS
 -Returning them (Have pity)   42

SINGING
 -In public (Save us)   43

SPITTING
 -In public (WHAT?!?)   44

THEATRES
 -Talking (Stop it)   45

TIPPING
 -Amount (Cheapskate)   46
 - Housekeeping staff (Share the wealth) 47

TRAFFIC SIGNAL
 -Blinking red light (We all stop)   48

TABLE OF CONTENTS   RULE #

TRASH
    -Disposal (I am not your mama)   49
    -Incorrect disposal (I am not your maid)   50

TURN SIGNAL
    -When to use (Always on time)   51

WALKING
    -Picking up feet (Laziness is not cute)   52

INTRODUCTION/EXPLANATION

There are so many wonderful cultures on our planet. This IS a great blessing. Fortunately, because we all are innately communal as humans, one problem that can easily be corrected in our society is the concept of people being on the same page as far as the "society's getting along rules" are concerned. This problem has become more noticeable since most industrialized nations no longer have such closely connected (distance-wise) extended families. Rules are no longer passed on and consistently reinforced in our society the way they used to be.

In addition, since the majority of us are so concerned about being politically correct and our parents and grandparents do not live nearby anymore to nag us, no one helps us learn the societal rules of cooperation. No one is ALLOWED to confront us on what is right and/or wrong.

We are taking up this challenge by presenting this book as a start to a more harmonious future. Getting along is in the best interest of our communities, cities, states, country, and the world.

Our weakest link should not be something that can be so easily remedied by a couple of sentences which will allow us to agree on a consistent cooperation agreement. So let's get started here and now!

DIRECTIONS FOR READING THIS BOOK

This book will present 52 suggestions (for the politically correct but the rest of us know them as rules). This will allow one rule for each week of the year. We decided this because we realized that "good" rules need time to be learned, practiced, and mastered. Too many suggestions at one time would be overwhelming and discouraging. We want people to actually apply what they are reading. This book is meant to be a self and societal improvement book. It is important to practice the behavior as often as the situation occurs in your life.

There are four sections on each page of rules. The first section on the page is called KIND WAY. This is for the fantastic folk reading this book who want to cooperate in society so that this lifetime will be a more calm, productive, and joyful place to be. Fantastic folk will read, learn, and practice the rule immediately. The only reason fantastic folk were not following the rule before was solely because they just did not know it. Now that they know it, they will follow it to the very best of their ability!

The second section is called PRIOR LOWER THOUGHTS. This part of the page puts into written word what we used to think before we understood that our former behavior was not good behavior.

The third section is called HIGHER THOUGHTS. This section puts into words what we think now that we understand that our former bad behavior was not correct. It oftentimes will explain why this new behavior that we are, of course, now practicing makes sense.

Finally, the fourth section is called SKULL (short for skull and cross bones). Warning: PLEASE do NOT read the SKULL section unless you are one of the hard-to-reach learners. These are the people who need extra convincing to do the right thing. We put this section in only because we were informed that some people (the hard-to-reach ones) are not used to being spoken to in a nice and politically correct fashion. We were warned that the only way for some folk to really want to change their behavior was to see down and dirty VERY earthy wording. We did NOT use curse words, per se. But it is still not pretty talk.

READY, SET, BEGIN!

#1 AGE

Kind way:
Please remember: Say "Eighteen" whenever you attempt to guess anyone's age in their presence.

Prior lower thoughts/words/behavior:
I know you are thinking, "Whom is he/she trying to fool! They know everyone is going to get older, not younger! I hate playing these age games with people! If I tell them they look their "real" age instead of the age they are fantasizing in their deluded imagination then it is a needed reality check. (HELLO, WAKE UP!)"

Higher thoughts:
It is best to NEVER guess someone's age. Feelings always seem to get hurt, but if you, for some strange reason, must attempt to guess someone's age, then eighteen appears to be the perfect "age number." (All folk--younger and older than eighteen--seem to want to look old enough to be legal but still be an even-numbered teenager's age with all the "sassy" that seems to imply.)

Skull:
Don't even go there! It is way too risky to talk age. Anyone whose self-esteem is so low that they ask someone to guess their age (unless it is that win-a-prize game at the carnival) needs to stay away from the rest of society. Their ego issues make them dangerous. Anyone who attempts to guess someone's age, without being asked to do so, has a long way to go to even advance to the sensitivity level of caveman/woman.

#2 ANIMALS/PETS

Kind way:
Please remember: Do not allow your dog to continuously bark outside anytime but especially at night. Barking is for EMERGENCIES only.

Prior lower thoughts/words/behavior:
That's what dogs do, they bark. Get over it! Besides, my dog doesn't bark THAT loud. What do you want ME to do about it? You must hate animals or something! I don't even hear it anymore. You'll get used to it, too.

Higher thoughts:
This disturbs your neighbors' peace and sleep. Besides, if your dog barks for every little thing, no one will know when a REAL problem is happening.

Skull:
Listen, you live in a society with other people in it besides you. Learn to get along. If you let your dog bark at any time, except emergency situations, you are probably a person who does not clean up after your pets AND you probably play your music too loud, too.

#3 ANIMALS/PETS

Kind way:
Please remember: Always clean up your pets' fecal matter.

Prior lower thoughts/words/behavior:
I'm not going to pick up that nasty-smelling crap! That is what the dirt on the ground is for! Besides, it is embarrassing to pick up poop!

Higher thoughts:
People walking, jogging, and especially children playing may accidentally step, run, and even sit in that waste (which is full of disease, by the way).

Skull:
If you are not going to pick up your animals' crap then make sure you walk your pet in your house where YOU are the only one who has to deal with it instead of inflicting the rest of us with it.

#4 ANIMALS/PETS

Kind way:
Please remember: Neuter/spay your pets.

Prior lower thoughts/words/behavior:
I don't want to take away their joy by taking away their ability to reproduce.
I wouldn't want anyone to do that to me.
It is not natural to spay/neuter animals.
God will provide for all the animals born.
I want to make money by selling the baby animals.

Higher thoughts:
Since we have the wonderful gift of reducing the extreme amount of unwanted new animals by neutering or spaying, then we can stop the millions upon millions of deaths of animals that occur EVERY year because of pet overpopulation.
Neutered or spayed animals live longer, are healthier, and are more content. We will know we have done our part to reduce the killing of animals that must be executed because there are too many cats, dogs, etc. on this planet.

Skull:
You superstitious, scared, selfish animal executioner!!! For EVERY new kitten, puppy, etc. that you allow your cat, dog, etc. to create, just realize that YOU are responsible for the horrible death of at least that many animals. These poor animals must be drained of life because YOU refuse to take the time and/or energy to LEARN what is the truth of what is best for your companion animal as opposed to your "IQ equal to your shoe size" guessing. Grow up and do the CORRECT thing for your pet and the planet!

#5 ARGUING

Kind way:
Please remember: Never argue in public with spouse, friends, children, or anyone for that matter.

Prior lower thoughts/words/behavior
You think what you said was loud? You haven't even HEARD loud yet!!
I want everyone to hear me put you in your place in public, in private, and I don't care where.
I pay my taxes--I should be able to argue and yell anywhere I want.
What are you looking at?!!

Higher thoughts:
What goes on between me and someone else should stay between the two of us. It is nobody else's business. I will not disturb anyone else with my personal issues. It is not all those other people's fault. I will not allow myself to stoop so low as to argue in public. I am better than that.

Skull:
If you argue in public you are nothing but some kind of lowlife, trashy, ignorant child. You don't deserve to be allowed in public with the rest of the civilized people. If your mother and/or father did not teach you better manners than that, then you need to be kept in your room until you realize that the world does NOT revolve around you, you birdbrain!!

#6 ATM

Kind way:
Please remember: Take all paperwork with you after your transaction. Please do NOT throw anything on the ground or leave the receipt in the machine.

Prior lower thoughts/words/behavior:
Someone will pick it up--that's HIS OR HER job. I see that other people threw their junk down here so I'm not the only one. I'll just empty my ashtray here, too, while I'm at it. It will give someone some work to do.

Higher thought:
Always leave a place nicer (or at least no worse) for your being there than it was when you arrived. You may not be able to make other folk do the right thing but you do have the power to make your own behavior the best.

Skull:
Keep your pigsty lifestyle at home along with the rest of your antisocial behavior!

#7 ATM

Kind way:
Please remember: Stay at least one full van-length away from a person using an ATM.

Prior lower thoughts/words/behavior:
If I get right on their bumper it will make them hurry up. I am in a hurry. People are so DANG slow at these ATMs.

Higher thoughts:
This distance allows people to feel safe and secure while completing their transactions. It will, of course, be a quick transaction since I am sure they already know the sixty seconds at the ATM machine rule.

Skull:
Back your stupid car up and give the person at the ATM some space!! Especially knowing how things are in the world (unless, besides being a pushy-pig, you also live under a rock and are oblivious to how high the crime rate is nowadays). I bet you are the kind of person who has the nerve to get offended and have an attitude when someone looks at you with suspicion when you pull up close to his or her car.

#8 ATM

Kind way:
Please remember: Have all your paperwork completely filled out BEFORE you get to the automatic teller machine.

Prior lower thoughts/words/behavior:
I'm not going to get out of line and go around. I did not have an envelope so the folk behind me will just have to WAIT until I get done. There are other banks if they are in that big a hurry. They'd better not try to rush me because I'll go even slower then. I've got my rights!

Higher thoughts:
Since everyone is stressed and multitasking, it is best to keep a couple of extra ATM envelopes in your glove compartment so you can always fill it out BEFORE coming to the bank. No one should have to wait behind someone who is going to take more than sixty seconds at the automatic teller machine.

Skull:
If your life is in such chaos that you cannot even remember to have a bank envelope in your car then you deserve having to get out of line and go back around! Maybe that will help you to remember the next time! Get your life organized, buddy!!

#9 BABIES/CHILDREN

Kind way:
Please remember: Always accompany children under the age of fourteen to the restrooms or snack areas of public areas (i.e. movies, restaurants, etc.)

Prior lower thoughts/words/behavior:
If they don't get back here in ten minutes I'll go look for them. They will do the right thing because they know if I find out they were doing the wrong thing, I'll beat the "beeboop" out of them. They've got at least enough brains to go to the lavatory/snack bar and come back. Besides, I've seen lots of security guards around. Those kids can ask security if there is a problem. Why should I have to get up? I can see the lavatory from here. I'll see if they are acting up.

Higher thoughts:
Children will be children. Your supervision helps children learn the correct behavior to adjust and be a productive, not a destructive, part of society.

Skull:
Get up off your lazy "my child was an accident" rear and make sure YOUR children, that YOU (not the security guard) chose to have and keep, follow the rules of civilized society. Children should not be holding up the snack bar line, figuring out what they do or do not want, without you. Children should not be allowed to leave tissue/towel paper and unflushed toilets just because no one is directly watching them.

#10 BABIES/CHILDREN

Kind way:
Please remember: When giving compliments to parents about their babies/children, do not give more credit to one parent over the other. Make sure you give credit to both parents equally.

Prior lower thoughts/word/behavior:
Your baby is sooo cute! He/she looks so much like your husband.
I don't even like kids much, so you should be glad I said anything nice about your child.
I am so tired of being politically correct. Just be glad I don't tell you the negative truth about your kid.
There are too many brats in the world anyway. You should not have had your own biological one so you should be glad to get any kind of a compliment from me!

Higher thoughts:
Each parent wants to be acknowledged for being part of the creation of his or her offspring. To notice one parent as more involved, better looking, smarter, etc. than the other by noting a wonderful quality in their child and giving credit for it to one and not the other parent, is actually an insult to the parent who is not included in the compliment. It is better to give a mutual compliment that includes both parents.

Skull:
If after reading this you continue with this rude behavior of saying ignorant stuff that compliments one parent and, therefore, slaps the other in the face, we will know you don't really like children (or their parents) anyway and this is your way of doing some cowardly, passive-aggressive sniping crap. Grow up!!

#11 BABIES/CHILDREN

Kind way:
Please remember: Don't allow your babies/children to crawl on public floors.

Prior lower thoughts/words/behavior:
Sure, put the baby on the floor. I used to crawl on grocery store floors when I was a baby and it didn't kill me.
I am so tired of carrying this child around. I am going to let him/her crawl around on this church floor for a while to give my arms a break.
Crawling on the floor will make that baby strong and get her used to dirt. It will help build up the immune system.

Higher thoughts:
I have no idea what was on the bottom of the shoes of all the people who have been walking around on this floor so I will not allow my child to crawl around here. Children are so full of energy. They can easily put who knows what dirty, yucky thing that they find on the floor into their mouth and eat it before I get a chance to see it and take it from them.

Skull:
Look at the bottom of your shoe right now. What IS that stuff!!??? Then think of all the things you have ever stepped in while walking. Well, that is the same CRAP (hundreds of times over) that ends up on other people's shoes that then ends up on the floor that you are allowing your baby to crawl around in! What is that brown thing that your child just popped into his/her mouth that he/she just picked up off the floor that he/she was crawling around on?!?? Wake up, parents!!!

#12 BABIES/CHILDREN

Kind way:
Please remember: Never ever curse at or around a child.

Prior lower thoughts/words/behavior:
That little xxxxx is so xxxxx stupid!; he/she doesn't understand any xxxx thing other than me talking to him/her like this!! If that xxxx acted right I wouldn't have to talk to him/her like this. He/she'd better be glad I don't beat that xxxx instead of just cursing at him/her.

Higher thoughts:
Cursing models poor parenting skills to our children and can cause your children future psychological upset. It is also distracting to the community around you and can be an embarrassment to yourself, your home, and your family. Curse words are actually a symbol of powerlessness and a limited vocabulary. There are many classes, support groups, and organizations that will be glad to help you with parenting skills.

Skull:
Cursing at your child?! What type of uneducated, out of control "why don't they make parents get a parenting license before they can have children" person are you?! No child deserves to be treated like that. That child is only what you trained him/her to be. With that line of thinking then, the person who deserves the cursing is you (the parent).

#13 BABIES/CHILDREN

Kind way:
Please remember: Make sure that your children know their home address, phone number, and parents' full name as soon as the child can talk.

Prior lower thoughts/words/behavior:
I don't have time to teach those little crumb-snatchers all that information. I'm too busy.
Besides, they might tell that information to people who should not have it.
What do you mean they don't know that info?!!! They come into this same house every single ding-dong day!

Higher thoughts:
It is amazing how many times a child will get ill at school, or a parent is late picking them up with no explanation. Also, the information on the official record is incorrect or out of date. The child has NO idea of an address or phone number AND only knows that the parents' name is Mommy or Daddy.

Skull:
Obviously, you do not want your child to find you. That is why you did not change the contact information and you did not bother to teach your child this information. Or maybe you are into some shady dealings that you cannot afford to have anyone track you down? I would, of course, not want to assume you are just a knucklehead!

#14 BABIES/CHILDREN

Kind way:
Please remember: Avoid bringing a baby/small child to a religious service geared toward adults.

Prior lower thoughts/words/behavior:
What are you looking at! You were all babies once yourselves. I'm sure you've heard a baby cry before. You know I can't make a baby stop crying when it starts. I'm tired! It's not THAT loud. I can't afford a babysitter. What kind of church people are you if you have an attitude about babies!

Higher thoughts:
Others cannot hear the service when a baby is crying/making noise. Suggest a childcare service be offered at your place of worship and make sure your child is one of the customers of that service. Another choice (if two persons are available to help with child rearing) is choosing two different times to attend service (or two different churches if your church only offers one service). Each of the adult persons attends service alone while the other adult, left at home, takes care of the baby/children.

Skull:
Not everyone thinks your child is CUTE. You nor the baby/child (nor the people around you) are getting anything out the service when a baby/child is being distracting. If none of the above ideas work, then try watching church service on TV or listening to it on the radio until some other socially enlightened option comes up or until your child grows up.

#15 BABIES/CHILDREN

Kind way:
Please remember: Avoid taking a baby to a movie theater.

Prior lower thoughts/words/behavior:
I need this time for me. Besides, babies get in free. They must have known babies cry before they wrote that. My baby will stop crying in a minute--she always does. I'd leave the theater but I already paid for the ticket and they won't refund my money so I'm staying no matter how loud my baby gets. I'm going to get my money's worth.

Higher thoughts:
Babies usually end up making noise, which disturbs you, and the other moviegoers around you. A crying baby causes everyone to waste his or her time and money in an unhappy, unpleasant experience.

Skull:
Get that crying kid the HECK out of the movie theater!! If you aren't bright enough to figure out that little bit of information, then you do NOT need to be raising children.

#16 CHURCH

Kind way:
Please remember: Never talk during a church service unless the church ritual calls for talking.

Prior lower thoughts/words/behavior:
If I whisper low enough no one will hear me.
I've got a great joke to tell and I'll forget it if I don't tell you now. Besides, jokes are so much funnier in church when you are not supposed to be talking!

Higher thoughts:
If communication is absolutely necessary for an emergency of some sort, write a brief note to that other person.

Skull:
If you are not going to church for the sole purpose of worshipping God then keep your noisy heathen rear at home!!!

#17 CLOTHING

Kind way:
Please remember: Don't wear bedroom slippers outside of your home.

Prior lower thoughts/words/behavior:
They are comfortable.
Get a life.
Mind your own business.
Are you going to buy my clothes for me?!

Higher thoughts:
Bedroom slippers do not protect your feet from glass, nails, rocks, dirt, etc. Normally while wearing slippers, we have a tendency to scuff our feet while walking, which wears the shoes out very, very quickly. They also leave an impression that the wearer is not as productive as the average person, if you know what I mean.

Skull:
Were you raised in the pigs' stall? What kind of upbringing would EVER say to you let me look like the dirtiest, laziest person ever born. Let me wear my bedroom slippers, that, as the name implies, I am supposed to wear in the bedroom, into the streets of real society. This way real society will know I am so danged dirty and lazy that I am not even going to expend the energy it takes to bend down to put on some real shoes to protect my feet (and I will probably try to sue someone when I hurt my stupid lazy feet, by the way). Then I am going to take that nasty dirt and grime from the streets right back into my bedroom!! YUCK!

#18 COURTESY

Kind way:
Please remember: When someone gives you a compliment, say, "How nice of you to notice and help build my confidence like that. Thank you."

Prior lower thoughts/words/behavior:
Don't give me a compliment; I never know what to say when people compliment me!
You are probably only trying to suck up anyway.
You don't really mean it.
Now I bet you are waiting for me to compliment you back.
I never think fast enough on my feet to think of something to say.

Higher thoughts:
Notice the act of kindness response gives an honest compliment back to the person who complimented you. It is nice that someone makes the effort to come outside of "self" long enough to notice something nice about another person. It also allows you to say THANK YOU without the need to disagree with the compliment that people have a tendency to do just to sound humble. Unfortunately, that type of "humble" response causes an uncomfortable situation in that the person giving the compliment is now forced to repeat and repeat the compliment.

Skull:
As crazy as the world can be, take the compliment, say "thank you," and run! Stop wasting everyone's time by denying the compliment. You know you love the attention. Don't make the other person sorry they ever tried to give you a compliment. You may never get another one from that person (or anyone else for that matter).

#19 COURTESY

Kind way:
Please remember: Watch from your door/window to make sure any visitor you have invited to your home or care for in any way, safely walks to his/her car and drives away before you continue with your other activities.

Prior lower thoughts/words/behavior:
Shutting the door as soon as their feet are on the other side of the door enough for you to close the door.
Close the door! Heck, it's cold out there!
You go back to watching your TV program. (You wouldn't even be able to hear them scream.)
You never even bothered to look back to see if they made it safely off the porch.

Higher thoughts:
It would be even better, especially if the visitor is alone, to walk them to their car or at least keep your house door open while they walk to their car. It can be a scary world out there.

Skull:
Keep your selfish, lazy (and probably drunk) butt at the door at least long enough to make sure your guests drive off safely. You can stay awake that short amount of time. Just be glad YOU are not the one who has to drive ALL the way home. You are lucky enough to be AT home. You didn't even have to use up your gasoline to visit yourself.

#20 DOORS

Kind way:
Please remember: If someone is within ten feet or less of a door, wait and hold the door open for him/her.

Prior lower thoughts/words/behavior:
What am I, a doorwoman/man?
They've got two good arms.
I'm late. I don't have time to hold a door open for slow people.
They wouldn't hold it open for me!
I feel stupid holding the door open!
How many folks do I have to hold the door open for?! I could conceivably keep holding this door open forever.

Higher thoughts:
Random acts of kindness have a domino effect. I'm nice to you. You are nice to the next person and so on.

Skull:
Hey, knucklehead, open your eyes and see there is someone else in this world besides you!! If you are running late, then use this as a penance for dragging your feet, slowing yourself up, and not leaving home in time!

#21 DOORS

Kind way:
Please remember: Whenever anyone holds a door open for you, say "Thank you!"

Prior lower thoughts/words/behavior:
I didn't ask him/her to hold the door open. Why should I have to say "Thank you?!"
He/she SHOULD hold the door open for me. I deserve, at least, that and more, from the world.
He/she is probably trying to get next to me and since he/she is ugly I don't want to encourage that by saying "Thank you."

Higher thoughts:
Courtesy and gratitude go a long way to change the world we live in. With all of the negative behavior in this world that I complain about, I can at least acknowledge positive behavior for a change.

Skull:
Anyone who does not say "Thank you" to a person who holds the door open should be put on a desert island naked with a lot of thorn-laden cactus and broken glass.

#22 "DRIVEE"

Kind way:
Please remember: If you know someone has agreed to drive and pick you up always be ready AT LEAST ten minutes earlier than the assigned time.

Prior lower thoughts/words/behavior:
As cute as I am, they should know it takes me a long time to get ready so they will just have to wait. I am worth it and more.
I've got a lot of things to do so they just need to understand why I am late. Everyone is late.
I don't want to seem too easy, eager, or available.

Higher thoughts:
That driver should not have to wait or waste time. That driver is using his/her gas and vehicle. The least you can do is be on time.

Skull:
Being late is NOT cute. It is just a sign of being rude. Being late is also a signal that you must be lazy, bratty, selfish, and clueless (another way of saying stupid).

#23 DRIVING

Kind way:
Please remember: When you are driving and holding a conversation, do NOT look at the other person(s). Keep your eyes on the road at all times!

Prior lower thoughts/words/behavior:
If I don't look at the other person, I can't see if he/she is listening to me.
I need to see their facial expressions.
I need for them to see my facial expressions.
I always thought it was rude to not look at people when talking to them.

Higher thoughts:
It only takes a split second for a car, person, or animal to dart in front of your car or for someone to hit his or her brakes in front of your car. Now you have a tragedy on your hands.

Skull:
First of all, you look like a real nimrod talking with your head turning back and forth, back and forth. If you are someone doing that in the first place, let's face it, you are probably someone who needs to really concentrate on your driving and NOTHING else but driving. Multitasking is a bit over your (turning) head in terms of mental abilities.

#24 DRIVING

Kind way:
Please remember: Wait until there is a distance of at least two large bus lengths of space on dry pavement and at least three large bus lengths of space on wet pavement before merging in front of a truck (i.e. eighteen-wheeler).

Prior lower thoughts/words/behavior:
There's a truck. If I'm fast, I can whip in front of it. I only need a foot of space to sneak in.
Trucks are slow anyway. I will hurry and jump in front of it.
Trucks are use to people zigzagging in front of them. It is not a problem.

Higher thoughts:
You do not have to study physics to get an idea of how much weight trucks have to stop with their brakes. Remember, it takes several feet for you to stop your MUCH smaller, comparatively lighter vehicle. Multiply that weight and forward motion concept to get an understanding of how stressful it must be for a truck driver to have someone come out of nowhere suddenly and jump in front of his/her truck. Please have mercy!

Skull:
Anyone who does not leave enough space before pulling in front of any vehicle (much less a truck) should have to eat an entire truck tire in front of a football stadium full of people. You are someone who got your driver's license out of a Cracker Jack box. (I am just surprised that, with your lack of intelligence, you did not eat the Cracker Jack box license by mistake. And now that I think about it, it is too bad you didn't.)

#25 DRIVING

Kind way:
Please remember: Give a kind wave of your hand or three blinks of your hazard lights to any person who lets you merge when driving.

Prior lower thoughts/words/behavior:
I'm not going to wave at anybody. I don't know that person! He/she's probably a knucklehead. Besides, he/she didn't LET me in. I was going to get in whether he/she let me or not! They had no choice in the matter. Therefore, they did not earn a "kind wave."

Higher thoughts:
We are working on positive attitudes. It is like a domino effect. One kind act leads to another and another. Besides, with your new attitude I am sure you were not going to bulldoze your way into a spot!

Skull:
Another kindergarten lesson that you missed?!! You must have skipped a lot of kindergarten classes, friend. May I strongly suggest you return to kindergarten for, especially, that lesson on saying "Thank you?" You might as well stay for the lessons on saying "Please," "You are welcome," and "Excuse me," too. I am sure those will also be new concepts to you.

#26 DRIVING

Kind way:
Please remember: If you are the mergee (the one who is being asked to let someone in front of you), allow one car in front of you. If you are the merger (the one asking to get in front of someone), take your turn to merge ONE and only ONE car in front of the mergee.

Prior lower thoughts/words/behavior:
There's a sucker who let a car in. If I speed up really fast and push my way in, I can force myself in front of that same driver!
Let me in! You let those other ten cars in!
I am going to push my way in. My car is bigger than yours. You won't take the chance of hitting me and damaging your precious little car.
I will push my way in front of that car that just let someone in. They might be mad but who cares. Not my problem.

Higher thoughts:
If everyone takes his/her turn, then traffic and tempers will stay harmonious. (Please remember the kind wave and/or the blinking lights when you are courteously allowed to merge. These two kind acts are also explained and located in this book.)

Skull:
Don't be a pushy-pig. Wait your turn. Didn't you learn ANYTHING in kindergarten!! It would be great to make pushy-pigs go back to kindergarten and stay there until they finally learn this lesson. (It doesn't matter how many years it may take for that kind of pea brain to get it.)

#27 DRIVING

Kind way:
Please remember: When dropping someone off or picking him/her up (i.e. at a store, at the cleaners, etc), pull your car close to the curb area as possible.

Prior lower thoughts/words/behavior:
You all will just have to wait. I am dropping someone off and I should not have to get close to the curb to do that.
Make me move!!
I will only hold everyone up for two minutes. They can't be in that big of a hurry!!

Higher thoughts:
I will pull over as close to the curb as I can so that I do not hold anyone up. I know how I feel when I have somewhere to go and someone in front of me could pull over but doesn't.

Skull:
Move that hunk of junk over!! If only I had a tank, I would ride over the top of you and your pitiful car. This is NOT the Academy Awards. People have places to go, you pinhead! When you do not use that "brain" that is supposed to be in your fathead, then it disintegrates. That must be what happened to you!!

#28 EARS

Kind way:
Please remember: Avoid cleaning your ears in front of any other person.

Prior lower thoughts/words/behavior:
As long as I don't use my fingers, then cleaning my ears in public is A-OK. I use a cotton swab, ink pen, pencil, etc. That must be correct. I see a lot of people do it.
It is a free country. If they don't like it, they don't have to look!

Higher thoughts:
I am part of a society. I realize that MANY people are disgusted by someone else's body dirt. There are many places where I can go to privately take care of my hygiene issues. I have enough social skills and dignity to blend in with polite society.

Skull:
Who the H-E-double hockey sticks do you think wants to watch you digging dirty, nasty globs of wax out of your ears!!! Is there a brain up in that big head of yours? And I do not want to even imagine where you put that bacteria-ridden crud when you pull it out. You are the kind of person who will dig for potatoes in your ears with someone else's ink pen or paperclips and then put them back to be used, unknowingly, by some unsuspecting innocent person, with all those germs and dirt on it. You should not be allowed inside of a facility that has other people in it.

#29 EATING

Kind way:
Please remember: Do not talk with food in your mouth.

Prior lower thoughts/words/behavior:
I can't wait that long time it takes to chew and swallow before I talk.
I've got real important things to say.
I'm the smartest one at this table.

Higher thoughts:
When you talk while eating, more times than not, this can cause food to fly disgustingly out of the mouth and land on objects and even people (yuck). Also, remember, people have been known to choke the most often when they are eating and talking.

Skull:
Your "wisdom of the universe" (that is sarcasm in case you did not get it) can wait until your mouth is empty! Hey, "snort, snort" instead of STUFFING huge hunks of things in your mouth that take longer to get rid of (and you look like a hog when you do). Try cutting your food into smaller pieces. You can talk sooner then.

#30 ELEVATOR

Kind way:
Please remember: Always say "Hello" when entering an elevator that is already occupied.

Prior lower thoughts/words/behavior:
They should say something to me first. Why do I have to be the one to speak? If I say something that means I have to actually carry on a conversation with the folks on the elevator. I do NOT want to have to be obligated to do that for the next whole thirty seconds or so.

Higher thoughts:
Everyone is feeling uncomfortable having to be in such a small box with strangers. I will be the bigger person and break the tension by giving a kind greeting as soon as I enter the elevator. Besides, it will give these shy passengers something else to do instead of just watching the floor numbers change above the sliding doors.

Skull:
Just open your big fat mouth and say "Hello," especially since you know how it feels to be standing in silence inside of an elevator with shy people. You seem to love to be the center of attention when no one wants you to be. Try making your inappropriate energy work for something good for a change.

#31 EMBARRASSING MOMENTS

Kind way:
Please remember: Be kind enough to assertively whisper to someone that something is wrong and/or out of place. Please do not think that not saying anything is easier.

Prior lower thoughts/words/behavior:
How embarrassing! I am not going to be the one to get yelled at for telling someone that tissue is hanging out of the top of their slacks or that their shirt is hiked up and stuck in their pantyhose, etc.
Not my problem! I just thank God it is not me.
I never know what to say so I won't say anything.

Higher thoughts:
I am going to quickly and assertively call that person in the embarrassing situation out of the room and whisper privately to them the following, "I had to tell you because the same thing happened to me last week. No one told me that I had greens all in my teeth ALL day. I only wished someone had told me what the problem was quickly so that I could have corrected it as soon as possible."

Skull:
Stop being so afraid and selfish!! I know you superstitiously think that if you are not the one who tells the "embarrassee" that maybe you will not be the one embarrassed. Get over it!! You know you would want someone to help you out and tell you that you are in an embarrassing situation before you figure it out eight hours later. You know you would feel a bit better if you find out after ONLY fifteen people have seen you rather than after one hundred and fifty people have seen you being embarrassed. It has happened at least once to EVERYONE over the age of eighteen. We ALL know how it feels and have (too much) empathy for it. We will all live through it.

#32 GUM

Kind Way:
Please remember: Always wrap your chewing gum that you are disposing of before you throw it into a trash container.

Prior lower thoughts/words/behavior:
Don't push it. You should just be glad I am even bothering to put my old chewed gum into a trashcan at all. Normally, I would spit it on the ground. I am NOT going to bother myself with wrapping it up!! You want a bow on it, too (snicker, snicker)!!

Higher thoughts:
That one little piece of sticky, yucky gum is going to completely make an entire huge trash bag un-reusable, even if there is only a couple of nice clean pieces of paper in it.
I have often needed to retrieve an important paper, which was accidentally thrown away, from a trash container but could not salvage it because of an icky, dirty, sticky clump of gum ruining it.

Skull:
There is no excuse for not wrapping chewed gum before disposing of it!!! Please use that pinhead of yours to think, for a change. Small pieces of scrap paper are everywhere. Use them to wrap your gum! What planet were you raised on?!??

#33 LINES

Kind way:
Please remember: After the cashier/teller has given you your change and receipt, move to the side to get out of the way, as quickly as possible, so the next customer can be waited on. Do not carry on idle chitchat. Do not stand in the way of the next customer while you reorganize your wallet/purse.

Prior lower thoughts/words/behavior
I patronize this store all of the time. I deserve the right to take up the cashier's time joking around and telling her about my life no matter how many people are behind me.
Just a minute, just a minute, I need to make sure that all of my dollar bills are facing just the right way before I put them in my wallet. And I need to check to see if the cashier gave me any of those special lucky year 2000 coins before I let the next person be waited on.

Higher thoughts:
If I just move five feet away from the cash register then the cashier will be able to wait on the next person and keep the line moving. Yet, I will still be close enough to be able to get my wallet in order and straighten out my money. It is a win/win.

Skull:
Move your addled slow self out of the way!! You are holding up the line. You can talk to the cashier--who couldn't care less about you, by the way--at some other time when there are not other customers waiting. Just because you do NOT have a life does not mean that other folk do not have things to do.

#34 LIPS

Kind way:
Please remember: Keep your lips together so your lips do not hang in the open position when you are not actually using your mouth.

Prior lower thoughts/behavior/words:
I can keep my lips hanging open if I want to. Besides, I think it looks cute! I remember my family used to think it was cute when I was a child so I am sure it is twice as cute now.
I don't have time to remember to keep my lips together. It is a habit to have my lower lip hang down.
Who is it hurting that I let my lower lip hang down!!

Higher thoughts:
Since I always want to present myself in the most attractive and professional manner, I am going to unlearn that awful habit of allowing my lower lip to hang down. This way, my lips will always be together when not in use. Besides, this makes me look more sophisticated and far more intelligent.

Skull:
Put your lips together and KEEP them together. You do NOT need to make yourself look even MORE mentally lost by keeping your bottom lip drooping down!! Are you even intelligent enough to realize how stupid you look!! When your mouth is open like that, your looks say that your IQ is at least thirty points lower than it really is (and you canNOT even afford to look like that!).

#35 MUSIC

Kind way:
Please remember: Make sure that the volume of the music you play is never loud enough for anyone outside your car or home to be able to hear it.

Prior lower thoughts/words/behavior:
I want my music so loud that I can set off car alarms!
My music is the best.
See how BIG my speakers are?!!
These speakers say I have money!
I am somebody!
Look at me!!

Higher thoughts:
When your favorite music is too loud, then others cannot hear their favorite music. Or you might wake up someone's sleeping baby, or someone who has to go to work the next shift, or someone who is sick.
Besides, even famous musicians have warned about the dangers of hearing loss because of the extreme volumes.
You are a danger on the road because you cannot hear warning horns, screams, or sirens that let you know there is a problem on the road around you because of your loud music.

Skull:
Turn the volume down, dumb-butt. Yes, I said dumb-butt! Obviously, the volume has killed off too many of your too few brain cells. We all know you are hoping some "mating" partner will hear your loud music, be so confused by the loud music (or lose enough brain cells), that they will actually agree to go out on a date with you because they will not be able to hear how poorly you speak over the loud music.

#36 NAILS

Kind way:
Please remember: Avoid clipping your fingernails and (God forbid) your toenails in public.

Prior lower thoughts/words/behavior:
I've a few moments to kill, let me take out my clippers and cut my nails. What are you looking at?!??
This "little" nail clipping sound won't bother anybody.
Somebody will sweep up my nail pieces that I just put on the floor. I'm not going to get them up. That would be nasty.

Higher thoughts:
Now that I know better I will do better. I did not realize before now that a LOT of people are extremely bothered (read that as "grossed out") by someone cutting their nails in public.
Those nail clippers are very loud so I cannot hide what I am doing. I will wait until I am at home and by myself to do that.

Skull:
DO NOT leave your dead cells (nails) all over the place. As a matter of fact, those clippers will send those nasty, dirty nails flying uncontrollably everywhere. They could end up on the people sitting in front of you, next to you, etc. Who do you think wants to sit in the same area where your nails went flying? There are probably enough fungus, bacteria, germs, etc. under your nails to cause an outbreak of a disease. Keep those nails at home in a trashcan. Don't expose any other children or adults to that. And since I know you do NOT pick up the cast-off dead and germ-y nails that you leave on the floor, I realize I could end up with them ground into the bottom of my shoes, or a child (who does not know any better) may end up on the floor with them. There should be a law!

#37 PAGE TURNING

Kind way:
Please remember: Especially when using a book/magazine that does not belong to you, NEVER lick your finger to help you turn the page.

Prior lower thoughts/words/behavior:
No one will ever know that I was the one who left a wet spot in that book. I had to turn the pages, didn't I?!!??
A little wet finger won't hurt the book.

Higher thoughts:
Since this is not my book, I will treat it with the utmost care and respect. I do not want to leave any unnecessary marks or wrinkles in it from using my wet finger to turn pages. I will make sure this book is as nice when I return it as it was when I received it.

Skull:
Who do you think wants to have YOUR spit on the pages of the book they have to use!!?? Even if you are way too selfish to care that you are putting your germs, and whatever color food that was left in your spit after you ate something, on the pages. Also, think about the fact that YOU might just be putting "who knows what" into YOUR own mouth that you are getting OFF of the pages when you are turning them with your nasty wet finger and then sticking that finger back into your mouth to drag more saliva out to assault the next page's corner to turn it.

#38 PHONE

Kind way:
Please remember: When you answer the phone for a business, ALWAYS, as soon as you pick up the phone and put it to your ear, say the name of the company to identify what number the person has contacted.

Prior lower thoughts/words/behavior:
Hello??!! If they are so dense that they don't know whom they are calling that is NOT my problem!! I am busy! I hate it when the phone rings and I have to answer it.
Not my company! I'm not the one making the big bucks. I couldn't care less how I sound over the phone.

Higher thoughts:
I represent this company when I answer the phone. If this company does well, then so do I.
My greeting is the first impression everyone gets of this company and me. I want to make it an excellent greeting.
It is not the fault of the person on the other end of this phone that I am not having a good day. I will not punish them. I know I do not want anyone to answer the phone when I call without letting me know which company I have contacted.

Skull:
Let's face it, you have millions of things to say (long and loud) when you are talking too much about nothing with your friends and family on the phone (and you are willing to do that for free). But you decide to get an attitude and use less than the minimum amount of words at your job! What sense does that make? And to make matters worse, you are even being paid. (This is your bread and butter, people!!!) If that company does not do well because

customers are not drawn to your company by the telephone impression you leave with them, then hopefully you will be the FIRST one fired as the company ends up having to cut jobs. "If you are not part of the solution, then you are part of the problem!" Nobody needs more problems. So please, either do your job or get out of the way.

#39 PHONE

Kind way:
Please remember: Always shut off or silence your cell phone and/or pager whenever you enter a theater (movie or live), classroom, seminar, meeting, etc. even if not directly asked to do so.

Prior lower thought/words/behavior:
I am so special that I cannot afford to have my cell/pager off.
Everyone has his or her phone on.
Look at me! I have a cell phone and I am popular because I get calls!!

Higher thoughts:
It is really rude of me to interrupt others with my phone ringing and with my one-sided conversation.
It is also rude of me to have a person in front of me whom I totally ignore in order to have a one-sided conversation with someone else. That is no fun for the person(s) around me.

Skull:
Get over yourself, butthead!! This world WILL continue to rotate on its axis if you shut off your cell phone. Of course maybe the inconclusive research is true and you have actually killed off a lot of your brain cells from holding your cell phone up to your head so much, especially the brain cells that hold your knowledge of courtesy.

#40 PHONE

Kind way:
Please remember: Whenever you leave a phone number as part of a message on a voice mail/answering machine, speak slowly and over-emphasize the enunciation of each number. Also, repeat the phone number two times AND say the phone number at the BEGINNING of the message.

Prior lower thoughts/words/behavior:
I am going to talk as fast as I can on that answering machine. It makes me sound smart. I do NOT like talking on those things. I sound terrible on those voice mail machines. They are such a pain in the behind. Besides that, "so and so" should be near the phone so I can talk directly to him/her. The world revolves around me, you know!

Higher thoughts:
I know how hard it is to hear voice mail messages clearly so I will try my best to make sure the message is as clear as a bell. That is what I want others to do when they leave me a message. It is so frustrating for the listener to not be able to clearly hear a phone number. The good thing is even if I make a mistake and cause the number to be hard to hear, I have repeated it and between the number being said two times, one of them will be clear enough to make out all of the numbers. Also, since I said the phone number at the beginning of the message, the listener will not have to listen to the entire message again and again to be able to find and replay the phone number.

Skull:
Obviously, you do NOT want someone to call you back! If you are not willing to make your call back number clear then PLEASE do not waste my voice mail

space pretending that you DO want me to call you back. Stop leaving some phone number that is garbled and fast. And especially, do not leave me a long butt message with the phone number buried somewhere in the middle of it that I have to search by replaying it to find it. What an inconsiderate and irritating thing to do. If you plan to continue that behavior, then DO NOT CALL AT ALL.

#41 PHONE

Kind way:
Please remember: When making a phone call and you reach a wrong number, say, "I am so sorry for disturbing you! Is this (repeat the number you were trying to dial)?" This is so you will know whether you HAVE a wrong number in your possession or if you just DIALED it incorrectly.

Prior lower thoughts/words/behavior:
Just hang up (and bang the phone down loudly).
Dial the number back two or three more times just to make sure you didn't dial the number wrong.
Or you used to think, *This voice sounds like that b**** or son of a b****. He/she is not going to get rid of me that easy!!*
Or you used to say, "Are you sure?!"
Or you used to say, "Well, you have a nice voice. Maybe YOU'D like to go out with me!"

Higher thoughts:
I know how it feels to have someone call my phone number accidentally. It can take up precious time. I will be extra courteous for the mistake I have made and not hold anyone up who states I have gotten him or her on the phone in error.
Or you will think, *Well it was worth a try. Better luck next time. That person obviously was not the one for me.*

Skull:
Wake up and pay attention to the numbers you dial!! If you do happen to get a wrong number, then you should be begging the person's forgiveness whom you have disturbed and begging nicely!!! You KNOW that you get an attitude

and a half whenever someone gives you a wrong call. That "do unto others" idea is more than just a notion! By the way, if somebody gave you a wrong number to get rid of you don't make yourself even more pitiful by trying to pick up some other stranger sight unseen. That is too sad!

#42 SHOPPING CARTS

Kind way:
Please remember: Return your shopping carts to the cart-return area. Please do not leave them in the parking lot driving area.

Prior lower thoughts/words/behavior:
Someone else will get this cart. That's what they get paid for. I don't have time to return it.
With all the money I paid at this store, the least they can do is come and get this stupid cart.
That cart-return area is too far away. I don't want to walk way over there to put this dumb cart back.

Higher thoughts:
This cart will end up in someone's way if I just leave it here. I will put it in the cart-area instead. That is what I would want others to do.
I know how irritating it is to have someone leave a store cart in a parking space that I wanted to use. It is always so crowded that it really holds people up when I have to leave my car to move a misplaced cart before I can park.

Skull:
I bet your mom still picks up after you!! At least try to pretend that you think about something/someone else besides your own egomaniac (look it up, stupid) self. There ARE other folk on this planet, you selfish creep! Walk that extra twenty feet to return the cart, you lazy, lazy idiot.

#43 SINGING IN PUBLIC

Kind way:
Please remember: Avoid singing in public places unless you are hired to do so or unless you are at a karaoke bar.

Prior lower thoughts/words/behavior:
I KNOW I can sing!!! I want to share my gift with the world!!
Listen to me!!!
My boyfriend/girlfriend/husband/wife/father/mother is always telling me how good my voice is!!
I sing in the volunteer choir. I know I sound good. I sing for the Lord.

Higher thoughts:
I will save my gift of singing for people who have actually asked me to sing. It is not my right to force anyone to hear me sing who did not make that request. They might have a headache or something that will not allow them to tolerate any extra sounds in their environment.

Skull:
If you are not Whitney Houston, Babyface, Sam Harris, Barbara Streisand, Mariah Carey, etc., do NOT, I repeat do NOT sing out in public when the entire group of folk around you did not ask for you to. You do NOT, I repeat do NOT sound as good as you fantasize. People either want to get your money, jump your bones, don't want to deal with a bad attitude from you, or they are being too nice (or too mean) to tell you the truth.
Stop fooling yourself and stop hurting our ears by being in your fool's paradise thinking you can sing.

#44 SPITTING

Kind way:
Please remember: Never spit in public.

Prior lower thoughts/words/ behavior:
It will evaporate.
Everyone does it!
Nobody will notice.
It makes me look grown up to spit.

Higher thoughts:
I know that I look uncivilized when I spit in public. I will not do that again. I will not spit on the ground, in the grass, etc. because children and adults might accidentally walk in it. And children might play on the ground in that area and get that expectorant on them!

Skull:
JUST STOP IT!! JUST SAY "NO, NO, NO, HECKEY NO!!" Why should any other living being have to worry about accidentally getting your slop on their shoes or (God forbid) their feet?! We should not have to worry about our children or our pets getting your gunk on themselves just because you want to look "cool."

#45 THEATERS

Kind way:
Please remember: Do not talk during a movie, play, seminar, etc. unless it is during a break or intermission.

Prior lower thoughts/words/behavior:
I have some brilliant ideas that I MUST tell the person next to me right NOW!!
I am such a great comedian that I know I can make people around me laugh.
I MUST be the center of attention. Everyone likes that!
I paid my money; I have the right to talk through the entertainment if I want to and who is going to stop me!!!
I am NOT talking that LOUD. No one can hear me!

Higher thoughts:
I will wait until the entertainment is over to talk because I don't want to miss even one word of what is going on up on the stage.
I will not say anything during the performance because I do not want to disturb anyone else's enjoyment. They will not be able to hear everything if I am talking.
I have found that even whispering is way too loud, so I will hold off on my comments until the break.

Skull:
SHUT your frigging mouth!!! If I want to hear you I will attend YOUR performance when your name is on the marquis.
No, loudmouth, you are NOT funny or clever. You are just annoyingly noisy and someone needs to put duct tape over your mouth!!

#46 TIPPING

Kind way:
Please remember: Always leave at least a fifteen-percent tip for any waitress/waiter who is efficient and courteous.

Prior lower thoughts/words/behavior:
I ain't going to leave a tip. They make more than I do!
They already get paid. This is their job. I don't get an extra tip at my job!
I only have enough money for the food. Forget that tip thing.

Higher thoughts:
If I don't have enough money to give at least a fifteen-percent tip I will get a takeout order instead of taking up a seat.
I know that waiters/waitresses make much less than minimum wage, so they depend on these tips for their livelihood.

Skull:
If you would just put that last beer down, you lush, you would probably have enough to pay the fifteen-percent tip. If you do not have enough money to give a decent fifteen-percent tip, then you need to keep your poor, cheap rear at home. Food at home is much less expensive than at a restaurant.

#47 TIPPING

Kind way:
Please remember: When staying at a hotel, motel, or inn, that provides daily housekeeping for your room, leave a tip EACH morning for the cleaner. (The housekeeping staff person may not be the same one each day; therefore, the tip you normally would leave on your last day of say a two, three day stay may not be the person who cleaned your room all the other days at all.)

Prior lower thoughts/words/behavior:
I am not going to leave some maid a tip. That is her job!
I am leaving fifty cents on the last day of my stay. Let them fight it out among themselves. Not my problem!
If they want a tip, they need to become a waiter or waitress. I don't tip them either but I hear some people do.

Higher thoughts:
The housekeeping staff works very hard and deserves to have their own tip when they have to clean up after the huge yucky mess we made out of this room!!! The person who cleans my room may be a mother or father trying make an honest living to raise a child on the meager wages they receive. Since I have enough to be able to take a trip and stay in a hotel/motel, I made sure I calculated the cost of tips into my budget as part of the original expense of the trip.

Skull:
I am sure you have enough money for that booze and those cigarettes you drank up/smoked up that did nothing good for anybody (not even for your selfish behind). You, therefore, need to cough up the daily tip for the overworked, underappreciated cleaning staff who have to clean up your nasty, filthy room after you have trashed it, cheapskate. If you can't afford to leave a decent tip, then you need to stay at home and save up until you CAN afford a decent tip.

#48 TRAFFIC SIGNAL

Kind way:
Please remember: Always come to a complete stop at a blinking red traffic light and look in all directions before proceeding to continue driving.

Prior lower thoughts/words/behavior:
That red blinking light must be broken. It doesn't mean anything so I don't have to stop.
If it is blinking red on my side, it must be blinking red on everyone's side so let them stop. I don't have time.
If I drive fast enough, I can get through that light since everyone else is supposed to stop anyway.

Higher thoughts:
It is ALWAYS better to be safe than sorry, so I will make sure I stop just in case someone else does not know the rules. My life is worth stopping my car for five or ten seconds.

Skull:
Even if all you did was attend kindergarten, you learned "RED MEANS STOP!" That does NOT mean for everyone except for you, Mr. or Mrs. Pomegranate Seed Brain!! If you were napping or skipping school that day, let me repeat: "RED MEANS STOP!"

#49 TRASH

Kind Way:
Please remember: When you are out outside of your own home, please pick up anything you drop (on the floor, ground, etc.) even if you consider it to be trash.

Prior lower thoughts/words/behavior:
I will act just like I don't see it.
It is embarrassing picking up trash that I "accidentally" dropped on the ground.
People will think I am a garbage picker or something.
That trash just blows away anyway. I don't need to pick it up.
Only "trashy" people stoop so low as to bend down to pick up trash.

Higher thoughts:
If I make a mess I MUST clean it up.
Anywhere I go I will make that space a little nicer than it was by cleaning up my trash AND a little more.
I must travel on this earth kindly and gently. I have only borrowed this planet from my children and the next generations.

Skull:
That trash does NOT disappear into space, you fathead!!! Pick up your trash. Your mother should not have to pick up after you anymore. If you continue with the type of two-year-old-baby selfish behavior that allows you to drop garbage in inappropriate places and keep on walking, you need to be put in a cage so your behavior can be contained.

#50 TRASH

Kind way:
Please remember: Throw trash into an "official" trash container. Never throw anything out of your car onto the street, sidewalk, grass, ground, or into the air.

Prior lower thoughts/words/behavior:
No one will see me.
I don't want this junk in my car.
It's dirty around here anyway.
Someone will pick it up.
Not my problem where that crap goes.

Higher thoughts:
I would not want anyone to throw trash onto MY property so I will not throw trash on anyone else's.
I am the steward of this entire planet. I want to maintain the beauty everywhere I go. I want this planet to be a nicer place for my having been here.

Skull:
What kind of lazy skank polecats raised you???!!! YOU created that trash in your car. Now YOU need to dispose of it correctly! Just because you don't have the manners of a pack of sick wild dogs does not mean everyone wants to live in filth like you obviously do!! The laws should be changed so that anyone who puts trash anywhere besides an "official" trash container should be forced to pick up every bit of trash for at least two square miles. And if they complain, more miles will be added.

#51 TURN SIGNAL

Kind way:
Please remember: Before turning, changing lanes, etc. communicate to other drivers by giving the required signal with your electrical indicator or by using the appropriate hands signals. Start signaling at least half of a city block before you turn or change lanes.

Prior lower thoughts/words/behavior:
I pay my taxes. If I want to turn, I will just turn. I do NOT have to signal to anybody to let them know. Those people behind me will just have to wait. They will get over it. I am sure they don't use their signal either.

Higher thoughts:
When I turn my signal on early enough, that allows traffic to flow smoothly because people will have plenty of time to go around me. It also helps to avoid accidents because other drivers know I am getting ready to stop.

Skull:
There are other people on the road, you clueless idiot!! Let us know that you are getting ready to turn or move over. I know you THINK the world revolves around you and, therefore, we should be reading your every thought, but that is NOT the truth, brick-brain. We have no idea what you are doing next unless you signal that intention to us.
And by the way, if you are ever on a street with no designated left turn lane on it, do NOT sit at the red light (more than likely looking stupid) and then wait until the traffic signal turns green to pop your indicator on. If you do this, I will have to misuse my religion and pray that the person behind you, whom you are holding up, rams your car into next week.

#52 WALKING

Kind way:
Please remember: Pick up your feet (and avoid dragging/scraping your shoes) while you are walking.

Prior lower thoughts/words/behavior:
I'm so tired!! I am not going to even pick my feet up while I am walking.
I love dragging my feet because it makes me look cute.
When I drag my feet I get a lot of attention.

Higher thoughts:
I should always lift my feet when I am walking. It looks more professional. I avoid disturbing others around me because I am able to silently enter and exit any areas that I approach. I am able to cut down on the amount of times I trip on uneven surfaces on the ground. And I also save money on replacement shoes.

Skull:
Pick up your clod-like feet when you are walking. Do you have ANY idea how lazy, sloppy, and stupid you look dragging your feet like you have an IQ in the negative numbers or something!! If you want people to treat you like you have some intelligence, you need to act like someone who has (at least a little) intelligence.

AUTHORS' BIOGRAPHICAL INFO:

Garie Thomas-Bass, BA, EX, CX /1ST CLASS STATIONARY ENGINEER

Garie Thomas-Bass graduated from Cass High School in Detroit, honorary Phi Beta Kappa from the Performing Arts curriculum.

Mrs. Thomas-Bass graduated summa cum laude from the University of Detroit, where she earned her teaching certification in 1980. Her major was mathematics. Her minor was social sciences. Garie earned her Continuing Educational Certification from Wayne State University. She taught full time for eleven years in Detroit, Michigan.

She teaches mathematics at the Education Center of The International Union of Operating Engineers' Local 547 in Detroit one semester each year and has done so for the last nine years.

Presently and for the past fifteen years, Mrs. Thomas-Bass's full-time profession is as a stationary engineer. She is chief engineer, with a First Class steam license, at the Detroit Public School System.

Her varied background has afforded Mrs. Thomas-Bass the opportunity to observe human behavior with a social scientist's and educator's eyes. Being a teacher has made her a stickler for rules to provide an environment of order and safety for all of her students to learn to their greatest capacity. She realizes rules make the world a better place to live and learn in.

She is married to Paul Bass. Garie and Paul share their home with a wonderful kitty cat named "G."

Dr. Kertia (Thomas-)Black, MD

Dr. Kertia Black is a board-certified physical medicine and rehabilitation physician who is currently in practice at the Rehabilitation Institute of Michigan (RIM) in Detroit, Michigan. RIM is one of the few free-standing rehabilitation hospitals in Michigan and is noted for its comprehensive services and research.

Kertia received her BA from Wayne State University. Her MPS and M. Ed were earned from Cornell and Temple Universities respectively. Her MD is from Hahnemann University, School of Medicine. Dr. Kertia Thomas-Black has been on staff at RIM since 1993 and served three years as its chief of staff and vice president for Medical Affairs. She specializes in the treatment of patients with traumatic brain injury and stroke. Since 2003, she has also served as assistant dean for Student Affairs at the Wayne State University School of Medicine, also in Detroit.

Kertia is also the creator, writer and star of the award-winning cable television show in Southfield, Michigan, called *To Your Health*.

She is married to Sidney Black and has two adult children: Kareem, a professional photographer, and Christine, a college student.

Kirtis Thomas III, LLP LPC

His certification and licensure include: Limited License Psychologist--Michigan Licensed Professional Counselor (full license). He received his BA from Michigan State University (Psychology), and his MA and Post MA from Western Michigan University (Guidance counseling/Psychology). In addition, in 1986 he completed the Rorschach Testing Course at Mercy College.

In his twenty-six years of being a psychologist he has worked in many capacities, including independent contractor, therapist, staff psychologist, supervisor, and private practice. He has treated and/or evaluated over 10,000 patients.

His skilled and varied psychology background has afforded him many opportunities to observe and experience human behavior. This, in turn, makes him an excellent voice of authority for this type of rules-oriented writing.

He is married to Jeanne Thomas and they have many cats, dogs, and birds keeping them company.

Printed in the United States
105523LV00004B/104/A